glass +
glamour

EDITOR: Andrea Danese
PRODUCTION MANAGER: Maria Pia Gramaglia
BOOK & COVER DESIGN: Abbott Miller with Johnschen Kudos, Pentagram

This book was set in Neutraface by House Industries

Library of Congress Cataloging-in-Publication Data
Albrecht, Donald.
Glass and glamour: Steuben's modern moment, 1930–1960
Donald Albrecht, Marie McKee.
    p. cm.
 ISBN 0-8109-9118-7
 1. Steuben Glass, inc.—Exhibitions. 2. Crystal glass—United
States—History—20th century—Exhibitions. 3. Cut glass—United
States—History—20th century—Exhibitions. I. McKee, Marie. II. Title.
  NK5205.S75A4 2003
  748.29147'83—dc21

                                    2003007955

Printed and bound in Japan

Harry N. Abrams, Inc.
100 Fifth Avenue
New York, N.Y. 10011
www.abramsbooks.com

Abrams is a subsidiary of

glass +
glamour

Steuben's Modern Moment, 1930–1960

Donald Albrecht

Museum of the City of New York

Harry N. Abrams, Inc., Publishers

PREFACE ❋ On the occasion of the centennial of Steuben Glass, the Museum of the City of New York is pleased to present "Glass and Glamour: Steuben's Modern Moment, 1930–1960." The Museum welcomes the opportunity to showcase the art and artistry of Steuben, a company whose products have long been associated with the allure of New York City. "Glass and Glamour" tells the story of a time in the middle decades of the twentieth century when the modernist aesthetic seemed to offer a glimpse into a utopian future, when New York City's glamour was a metaphor for all things modern, and when glass became a medium of choice to express the vision of the avant-garde in architecture and design. ❋ In the midst of the Great Depression, Steuben made a bold move by deciding to link its image with that of New York City. The company relocated all of its design work to the city and, in 1934, opened its fabled showroom on New York's glamorous Fifth Avenue. For many New Yorkers in the middle years of the twentieth century, a trip to the Steuben showroom was as important a part of the cultural experience of Manhattan as a visit to Rockefeller Center or a ride on the Circle Line. ❋ As Donald Albrecht outlines in the essay that follows, the glass created by Steuben during the pivotal years from the 1930s to the early 1960s embodied New York sophistication. The company's artisans used traditional as well as new technology to produce brilliant, colorless lead-crystal tableware and decorative glass objects with sleek, uncluttered lines. Under the visionary leadership of Arthur Amory Houghton Jr., architect John Monteith Gates, and designer Sidney Waugh, Steuben forged a cutting-edge marketing campaign that sold New York glamour to people across the country. Owning a piece of Steuben, such as the 1942 Ship's Decanter, or the Olive Dish designed by John Dreves, became a symbol of exquisitely modern taste to which anyone could aspire. ❋ Steuben further enhanced the reputation of its commercial wares by highlighting magnificent one-of-a-kind or limited-edition artworks in a series of exhibitions in its Fifth Avenue showroom and in major museums in New York City and elsewhere. The 1940 "Twenty-seven Artists in Crystal" exhibition included works based on original drawings by such icons of mid-twentieth-century art as Henri Matisse, Isamu Noguchi, Georgia O'Keeffe, and Salvador Dalí. Such extraordinary projects built on and helped to reinforce New York City's stature as the cultural center of the twentieth century. ❋ The Museum of the City of New York is honored to mount a major exhibition highlighting some of the defining objects of Steuben's modern moment. Like glassmaking, an exhibition is a collaborative undertaking. This project was made possible through the generosity of many museums and private collectors, and the assistance of many people, including our colleagues at the Corning Museum of Glass and its Rakow Library, curator Donald Albrecht, project manager Peter Drobny, exhibition designer John Keenen of Keenen/Riley Architects, graphic designer Abbott Miller, Eric Himmel of Harry N. Abrams, and others. Marie McKee, president and CEO of Steuben Glass, and her colleagues have been ideal partners in this glittering endeavor.

Susan Henshaw Jones, director, Museum of the City of New York

In Steuben's Christmas catalogue for 1953, a model offers
Angus McDougall's iconic Apple.

FOREWORD ❋ Several years ago, when my colleagues and I sat down to begin planning a celebration of Steuben's 100th anniversary in 2003, we found ourselves focused not upon proof of how the company has profited and advanced, but upon the ways in which Steuben's vision remains constant. ❋ The world around us has undergone titanic shifts, of course, and Steuben's techniques for facilitating business have followed suit. There exists today, for example, a parallel universe known as the Internet, and our company is there. Steuben has more luxury retail partners, a different New York City flagship address, and an 800 number. However, in its core objectives and approach to making products, Steuben is little altered since 1933, when Arthur Amory Houghton Jr. assumed command of the company and introduced America to pure, colorless crystal designs created by a true artists' factory in upstate New York. ❋ Today, Steuben Glass is still a household name. We remain America's only maker of luxury crystal and purveyor of this nation's gifts of state since 1947. We still fashion both functional and decorative objects by hand, in relatively small numbers, in the same studios where glimmering tableware and home accessories, sculptures, commemorative pieces, and architectural elements have been made by foremost artists for decades. We continue to employ master craftspeople using the same tools—furnaces and hand-held iron implements—fundamental to an ancient alchemy that never ceases to amaze even us. We remain devoted to creating objects with the highest degree of combined purpose and pleasure. In our dedication to the integrity and materiality of glass itself, and in our intent to make things that express what they are, we continue to be stubbornly, optimistically committed to design excellence. ❋ If Steuben is the same in essence, what is there to celebrate in an era infatuated with radical change? The answer is simple. On the occasion of our centennial, Steuben celebrates the moment we became who we really are. The message of that moment—the modern moment explored in the exhibition this book documents—is that one object beautifully and sincerely made has the power to enhance joy in everyday living. Each piece of crystal Steuben creates contains within it a world we would want to inhabit and an expression of our confidence in the enduring relevance and transformative power of good design. ❋ On behalf of my colleagues, I wish to convey gratitude to curator Donald Albrecht, whose knowledge and insight have inspired us at Steuben. We are honored and delighted to be welcomed by Susan Henshaw Jones and the staff and trustees of the Museum of the City of New York, which is presenting "Glass and Glamour: Steuben's Modern Moment, 1930-1960." Steuben's current place in the history of American decorative arts would be quite simply unimaginable without New York City—the world's most potent wellspring of creativity, ambition, action, progressive thinking and, in the end, glamour.

Marie McKee, president and CEO, Steuben Glass

Steuben employees and guests socialize over cocktails at a reception
in the Steuben shop, c. 1959.

steuben's modern moment

Donald Albrecht

Light, transparent, and reflective, glass has come to represent the glamour of twentieth-century Modernism. As early as the 1920s and 1930s, houses made of glass in Paris, Berlin, Los Angeles, and Chicago promised an exciting new form of residential life by blurring the distinction between indoors and outdoors, machine and nature. After World War II, International Style steel-and-glass towers such as Lever House and the Corning Building rose in midtown Manhattan, captivating the public and forever redefining city skylines around the world. But the allure of glass was not confined to architecture. From studios in Austria, Finland, Italy, and other aesthetic centers, artists and industrial designers passionately embraced the challenge to create in the modern idiom. In the field of American glass that modern idiom was

The glass-block Corning-Steuben Building at 718 Fifth Avenue—housing
Steuben's shop, offices, and design studio—opened in 1937.

synonymous with Steuben.[1] ❄ Steuben's avant-garde decades coincided with America's own heady days of Modernism from the 1920s through the early 1960s, the celebrated era after World War I when progressive art and design symbolized the country's political and technological prowess. So compelling was the output of this formative era that contemporary taste is still being shaped by such midcentury icons as the fiberglass furniture of Charles and Ray Eames and the cool sophistication of Audrey Hepburn, dressed by Hubert de Givenchy, in *Breakfast at Tiffany's*. As Herbert Muschamp, architecture critic of the *New York Times*, recently wrote, "When I was growing up in the 50s and early 60s, everything modern seemed worth running after."[2] ❄ Steuben's modern times began in 1933. That year Arthur Amory Houghton Jr., a 27-year-old Harvard graduate and member of the family that controlled Corning Glass Works, decided to catapult the company's financially failing Steuben Division—later renamed Steuben Glass—into the realm of contemporary design. His timing was perfect. Like other innovators who adopted Modernism as a way to combat falling sales in the Depression (such as furniture manufacturer Herman Miller, Inc., which was revitalized by collaborations with Gilbert Rohde, George Nelson, and Ray and Charles Eames), Houghton not only reinvented his company but also launched a new chapter in twentieth-century design history. ❄ "Knowing we had skilled craftsmen . . . and a really beautiful composition for crystal," Houghton said he realized that "the needed elements were design and also how to sell the product."[3]

ABOVE: A receptionist at the 718 Fifth Avenue office is silhouetted against daylight streaming through the glass-block window-wall. LEFT: Three executives pause in front of the building's Fifty-sixth Street entrance.

John Monteith Gates (left), Arthur A. Houghton Jr., and Sidney Waugh—the suave Steuben triumvirate—confer over brandy and cigarettes around a table set with Steuben goblets and barware, c. 1934.

To achieve his vision to create an American glass that would vie with the best Europe had to offer, Houghton took the advice of leading industrial designer Walter Dorwin Teague to go modern and elite. Teague had worked during 1932 as a marketing consultant and tableware designer for Houghton's cousin and Corning president, Amory Houghton. Teague's shimmering "lens" bowls, faceted like automobile headlights, and his unadorned vases in Platonic shapes, selected by Philip Johnson for his landmark 1934 exhibition "Machine Art" at the new Museum of Modern Art, established Steuben's avant-garde credentials. Equally important, Teague claimed that through clever promotion and advertising Steuben could make its glassware "worth all we ask for it" and that owning Steuben glass would become "one of those evidences of solvency—like the ownership of a Cadillac . . . or a house in the right neighborhood."[4] It was an idea for branding Steuben that Houghton adopted wholeheartedly when he took over Corning's Steuben Division in 1933. ❄ Houghton quickly made his own mark on the new company. Teague's one-year contract had lapsed six months before Houghton took the reins at Steuben, and rather than revisit the relationship, Houghton elected to hire New York City–based architect John Monteith Gates as managing director and sculptor Sidney Waugh as design director. For three decades, the dynamic triumvirate of Houghton, Gates, and Waugh reshaped Steuben in a progressive "corporate" mode, envisioning their product through the multiple lenses of function, design, manufacturing, distribution, and promotion. Like

Herman Miller's furniture, Steuben's glassware was presented to the public in custom-designed shops, prestigious museum exhibitions, sophisticated advertising campaigns, and elegant publications. ❋ Houghton's commitment to modernism meant the abandonment of the ornamental frosted-, iridescent-, and colored-glass objects that had been Steuben's hallmark since the founding of the company in 1903. Instead, with some exceptions in the early 1930s, Steuben Glass would design and manufacture objects exclusively of a revolutionary clear-glass formula that Corning chemists had just developed for optical applications. A superior pure lead crystal called 10M, this new glass was unlike all previous crystal formulas. So pure that it did not require the addition of decolorizing agents, 10M was also the first glass to admit the full spectrum of light, including ultraviolet rays, giving it an extremely high index of refraction that gave every Steuben object a visual brilliance and unsurpassed clarity. ❋ Through the 10M formula, Steuben contributed to the modern movement's infatuation with new materials for the decorative arts. Glass in particular represented a progressive material that had undergone remarkable scientific and aesthetic transformations since the mid-nineteenth century. From Joseph Paxton's Crystal Palace built for London's Great Exhibition of 1851 to the glass-clad skyscrapers proposed by German architect Ludwig Mies van der Rohe in the 1920s, the transparency of buildings sheathed in large sheets of clear glass had come to symbolize a new free and open society. The Depression reinforced the utopian

Steuben's first New York shop, which opened in 1934, was located
at 748 Fifth Avenue. Sidney Waugh's illuminated crystal Gazelle
Fountain dominates a niche on the rear wall, while on the mezzanine
level, tablewares and pieces by Walter Dorwin Teague and Sidney
Waugh are displayed. Customers could also view architectural glass
panels, which had been produced at Steuben since the late 1920s.

ABOVE: Steuben's display occupied part of the Corning Glass Works exhibition space in the million-dollar Glass Center at the 1939 New York World's Fair, where products by Pittsburgh Plate Glass and Owens-Illinois were also on view.

RIGHT: The "Glass in the Home" exhibit at the World's Fair Glass Center, showing the dining room and living room. Much of the furniture itself is glass, including plate-glass chairs upholstered in a fiberglass material.

connotations of glass in the way that science and industry represented positive forces that would propel society to better economic times. Thus, in the 1930s, inventions like glass blocks and Thermopane windows reached the marketplace with great fanfare. Stores and magazines promoted the fashionability of glass clocks, bookends, desk sets, and radios. And visitors to the 1933–34 Century of Progress Exposition in Chicago marveled at the floor-to-ceiling glass walls of architect George Fred Keck's "House of Tomorrow," where the dining room table was set by Steuben. "The modern," *Arts and Decoration* magazine declared in 1934, "throws no stones."[5] ❄ With the hiring of Sidney Waugh, the characteristic Steuben look of the 1930s began to take form. Inspired by the restraint and simplicity of 1930s Swedish glass by Orrefors, these beautiful objects illustrate the creation of a signature style by Steuben designers characterized by weight and volume and adherence to the architectural principles of balance, proportion, profile, and scale. A prime example was Waugh's 1935 Gazelle Bowl, which juxtaposed an angular Art Deco base with a hemispherical bowl copper-wheel engraved with twelve graceful gazelles leaping in cinematic motion. Late 1930s and 1940s Steuben design was also defined by new glass interpretations of eighteenth-century models, from F. B. Sellew's Teardrop Candlesticks (with teardrop-shaped air bubbles trapped within their columns) to John Gates's 1939 Cream Pitcher with lavish curlicues. Concurrent with the public opening of Colonial Williamsburg, these designs updated

ABOVE: John Gates masterminded both merchandising and special exhibitions in Steuben's New York shop at the Corning-Steuben Building at 718 Fifth Avenue, including the dramatically illuminated "British Artists in Crystal" exhibition, which opened in 1954. RIGHT: The New Year's Bells window in 1950.

The shop at 717 Fifth Avenue. Steuben designer George Thompson's elaborate crystal Cascade Wall, reflected in a pool, divided the main sales room from the exhibition spaces and staff quarters beyond.

historical precedents through simplification and adaptation to the new glass and rode the contemporary wave of Colonial Revival fashion in America. ❄ Hewing to a tenet of the modern movement—truth to materials—many Steuben objects took on the naturally curvaceous shapes formed by hot, molten glass. Classics of this genre included John Dreves's 1939 Olive Dish and George Thompson's Galapagos Bowl of the same year. Presented to the public in Steuben's booth at the futuristic 1939 New York World's Fair, these masterpieces signaled a truly original Steuben style of simple, monumental bowls and other functional objects decorated with solid-glass bits that served as both ornaments and handles. "Massive enough to accentuate the inherent beauty of the material," James S. Plaut wrote in his postwar monograph on the company, "these pieces possess a delicacy and exuberance never in evidence earlier in Steuben's history."[6] ❄ Although Steuben objects continued to be handmade by glassblowers and artisans in Corning, New York, in the mid-1930s Houghton and Gates decided to start a design department in Manhattan. There, in the center of the nation's media, Steuben could strategically deploy the city's reputation for modernity and urbane glamour as a marketing tool. At the time, Depression-era Americans avidly followed the newspaper columns and radio broadcasts of Walter Winchell, anticipated the completion of Rockefeller Center, and delighted in viewing Hollywood's depiction of glass-walled Manhattan penthouses in popular movies. Steuben

In the July 1942 issue of *Vogue*, a glamorous Mrs. John Gates poses among crystal and flowers at Steuben's Spring Flower Show in the New York shop.

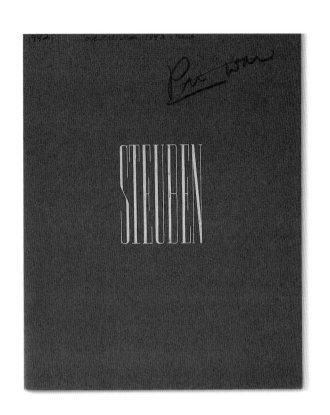

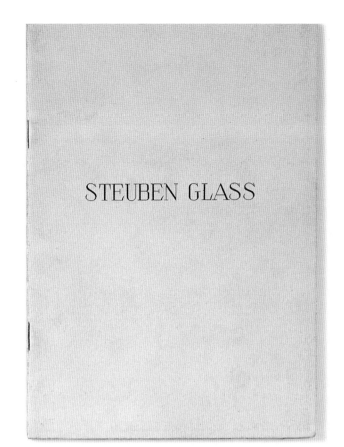

STEUBEN GLASS

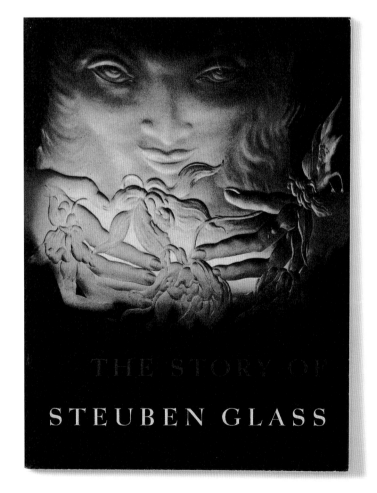

THE STORY OF
STEUBEN GLASS

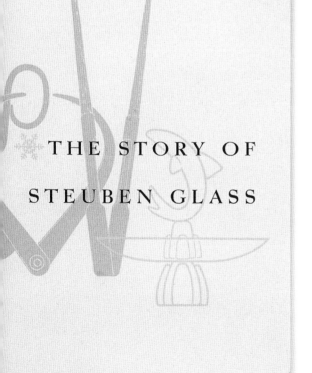

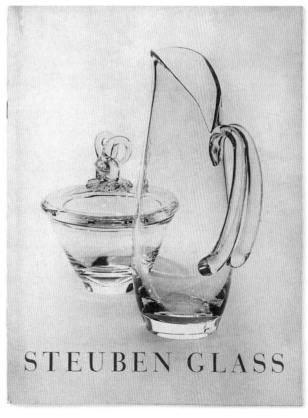

In the 1940s and 1950s, Steuben projected its modern image through distinctive sales brochures, books, and other publications, most designed in a distinctive graphic style by the Spiral Press.

capitalized on New York's charismatic Modernism in its design and marketing campaigns, presenting in 1942 the first of several "flower and crystal" exhibitions covered in *Vogue* and advertising in fashionable magazines and newspapers. This effort culminated in Steuben's 1957–1970s campaign in the *New York Times Magazine*, created by New York advertising guru David Ogilvy. ❆ In addition to assembling a design staff, primarily made up of architectural school graduates, Gates also launched a new permanent venue in New York to showcase Steuben's work. In 1934 Steuben opened its own shop at 748 Fifth Avenue, elegantly finished with silver gray walls and lustrous black rubber flooring. Designed by Gates with his former employer, the architectural firm of Charles A. Platt, and one of the leading Manhattan interior design companies, McMillen, the shop was a commercial temple—"a room," the *Architectural Forum* wrote, "in which to create desire rather than accomplish the definite sale."[7] In fact, the retail space featured no sales counters—instead, customers visited a special "display room" in the store to make their purchases. Then in 1937, as business expanded, Steuben moved to the new Corning-Steuben Building at 718 Fifth Avenue at Fifty-sixth Street, notable for its exterior walls of 3800 Corning Pyrex glass blocks set within panels of smooth Indiana limestone.[8] Influential critic Lewis Mumford praised the building's use of glass in the *New Yorker* magazine: "For the last ten

In the 1934 "Contemporary American Industrial Art" exhibition at the Metropolitan Museum of Art, Walter Dorwin Teague's Lens Bowl was shown (middle of lower shelf) along with some pieces of his tableware (top shelf, far left).

years I have conducted a campaign to persuade merchants to open up the interiors of their shops and to make the life within them the real show window. . . . The Steuben Glass shop on Fifth Avenue is a happy example. . . ."9 ❄ Also in 1937, Gates launched one of the company's most important design series and publicity events. Inspired by an encounter with artist Henri Matisse, Gates conceived the idea of commissioning leading artists to design a limited-edition series of vases, bowls, and urns. The result, "Twenty-seven Artists in Crystal," opened as an exhibition (launched by a white-tie party) in the new store in 1940. It presented works by a crosssection of internationally renowned American and European artists, whose specially commissioned drawings were engraved into glass by Steuben's master engravers. Although not a total aesthetic success (some of the work by painters was not ideally suited to copper-wheel engraving), the list of participants was impressive, from Matisse to Isamu Noguchi, Georgia O'Keeffe, Grant Wood, Thomas Hart Benton, Salvador Dalí, Giorgio de Chirico, Jean Cocteau, Raoul Dufy, Fernand Léger, and Paul Manship. Fusing art and industry—a major theme of the socially conscious 1930s— "Twenty-seven Artists in Crystal" inaugurated a Steuben tradition of commissioned series and was popular with the press and public. ❄ Twenty-seven Artists was Steuben's last hurrah before America's entry into World War II, when production and sales decreased and many

Salvador Dalí contemplates his Sleep of Nautilus, one of two commissions he created for Steuben. The second was a design for the "Twenty-seven Artists in Crystal" exhibition.

designers enlisted in the military. After the war, however, a new chapter opened for Steuben. Americans were now eager to spend, and virtually every industry responded with fresh designs and increased production. To accommodate the postwar need for more glassware, Steuben's design department expanded. A new generation of designers, including Lloyd Atkins, David Hills, and Donald Pollard, joined company veterans like George Thompson to bring Steuben's sophisticated brand of good living to upscale American homes and offices. New tableware and barware, from cocktail shakers to punch bowls, cigarette urns, cruets, and jam jars, grew from the prewar models created by Dreves and Thompson to become the iconic mainstays of Steuben production. With their distinctive aesthetic of elegant and disciplined sensuality, classic postwar designs featured biomorphic and abstract shapes, often accented by a single air-trapped teardrop or spiraling air-twist. (Air-twist ornaments were achieved by grooving a piece of glass, covering it with another layer so that parallel tunnels of air were trapped within, then twisting the glass to make the air tunnels spiral around each other.) In a spirit similar to the work of such postwar architects and designers as Gio Ponti and Alexander Girard, Steuben's glassware enriched the modern canon with decorative flair and visual invention. ❄ Steuben also achieved household name recognition during this period by actively pursuing a variety of promotional avenues. Its elegant

At midcentury, Steuben reinforced its brand awareness with a complete graphics and packaging program using gray flannel bags, hinged red-leather presentation cases, and stationery with the distinctive snowflake logo designed by Philip Grushkin.

publications and full-page advertisements, often appealing to "the privileged bride,"[10] were models of discretion, never soliciting, but inviting potential customers into the New York store with an alluring blend of luxury and practicality.[11] "Visitors to the Steuben Glass Shop," a 1960 *New York Times Magazine* ad read, "sometimes confess to a misgiving. Would they ever dare to use the dazzling things for such prosaic purposes as drinking water or snuffing out a cigarette? Their fears are groundless."[12] Once purchased, objects were wrapped in custom-designed flannel bags and monogrammed boxes. Equally important was the tacit endorsement of Manhattan celebrities, such as Leonard Bernstein and Richard Rodgers. By avidly collecting Steuben glassware or receiving Steuben-designed awards, they became unofficial ambassadors for the brand. ❄ Promotional activity centered on the company's flagship Manhattan store. Its seasonally themed displays attracted tourists from around the world, and it became a backdrop for highly publicized presentations of a new generation of artists' series launched in the 1950s. The series included "Studies in Crystal," the company's first exhibition of sculptural, non-functional designs, initiated in 1955, and a harbinger of Steuben's future direction. ("Asian Artists in Crystal," proposed by the U.S. government as a Cold War goodwill effort, was presented at the Metropolitan Museum of Art.) While displaying superb technical virtuosity, the series often

Using architecture to align itself with the contemporary idiom of New York, Steuben opened a shop on the ground floor of the new Corning Building at 717 Fifth Avenue at Fifty-sixth Street. It was the city's tallest glass-clad skyscraper when it opened in 1959.

Steuben's executive offices in the Corning Building at 717 Fifth Avenue
overlooked the company's 1937 glass-block structure across the street at
718 Fifth Avenue.

seemed to overreach for artistic effect. At the same time, trendsetting expositions of postwar contemporary design, most notably the Museum of Modern Art's "Good Design" exhibitions of the early 1950s, featured the company's functional stock pieces. ❄ As it had done with its glass-block building in the 1930s, Steuben deployed contemporary architecture as a way to align its products with New York's Modernism. Postwar New York was a metropolis undergoing a new "modernist moment." Like the rest of mainland United States, the city had emerged physically unscathed from World War II. Office towers, long a symbol of New York, broke new aesthetic and technical ground, launched by Skidmore, Owings & Merrill's 1952 Lever House. Its elegant glass shaft and gridded façade was followed by such structures as the Seagram Building and the Pepsi-Cola Building, which became optimistic symbols of an American-led world of international business and finance. Corning added its name to this list of the corporate elite in 1959 when its new headquarters, New York's tallest glass-clad skyscraper at the time, opened at 717 Fifth Avenue. Designed by Harrison & Abramovitz & Abbe, the building featured a Steuben retail store on the ground floor. Dominated by George Thompson's crystal Cascade Wall, comprising almost three hundred glass flowers with metal stamens that were reflected in a pool of water, the shop earned the praise of *Interiors* magazine as a "phantom setting for glass."[13] ❄ The opening of the new store coincided with corporate transformations at Steuben. Within a few years, the triumvirate that had conceived the company's midcentury designs and marketing strategy disbanded. In 1963 Sidney Waugh died, Gates retired in 1969, and Houghton stepped up to the position of chairman in 1973. During the 1960s, Steuben's design of overtly decorative objects, embellished with precious metals and jewels, veered from the earlier modernist emphasis on simpler, pure crystal tableware. ❄ While Steuben's aesthetic has changed since its modern moment, the company's effort to marry art and industry, function and beauty, glass and glamour forwarded the period's progressive agenda and remains today a vital chapter of twentieth-century design. Launched in a decidedly modern spirit of new beginnings, this moment also linked design to contemporary forms of media as well as to the era's ultimate modern metropolis, New York City. In the versatile hands of highly skilled designers and artisans, Steuben glass was fashioned in a range of styles, from streamlined olive dishes to fanciful Colonial Revival pitchers, neoclassical centerpieces, and cigarette boxes with Bauhaus purity. Steuben's stylistic variety was a physical manifestation of the malleability of glass itself, yet its repertoire was rendered new and modern by the crystalline clarity of the company's unique glass—a technological achievement that was invented in the optimistic mood of the mid-twentieth century. Steuben's iconic objects from the 1930s through the 1950s unequivocally achieved their early promise to be "as typical of our modern life as the skyscraper or the airplane."[14]

INDEX OF PLATES

Salad Bowl (6858), c. 1932
Frederick Carder*

Lens Bowls (7620), 1932
Walter Dorwin Teague
12", 18", 16" diameter

Brandy Balloons in various
sizes (7619), c. 1934

Liqueur Glass (7781), 1937
2³⁄₈" height

Air-Trap Vase (2254), 1948
John Dreves
8¹⁄₂" height

Whirlpool Vase (X564), 1939
Samuel Ayres
14¹⁄₂" height

Lotus Vase (X511), 1939
James McNaughton
15¹⁄₂" height

Heritage Cut Vase, 1939
John Monteith Gates
8¹⁄₂" height